Dates for the Greats

A PERSONAL ADS PARODY FROM ADAM & EVE TO SIGMUND FREUD

DORIS CHELMOW
& HAROLD RAND

Deborah Werksman, Publisher
Lysbeth Guillorn, Editor
Tom Greensfelder and Nicole Ferentz, Cover and Graphic Design
Nancy Moore Brochin, Proofreading and Copy Editing
Ellen Taylor, Word Processing
Barbara Kelly, Sales & Marketing

All photos from the Picture Collection–the Branch Libraries–New York Public Library
or the collection of the authors, except for:

Elizabeth Taylor as Cleopatra, Springer/Bettman Archive
Albert Einstein with the L.A. Citadel Band, Collection of Melvin Adelglass

Hysteria Publications is a book and calendar publisher dedicated to humor.
We'll gladly consider your manuscript or book proposal.
Please send submissions to:

PUBLICATIONS

Post Office Box 8581 - Bridgeport, CT 06605

Please include SASE and phone number with all submissions
and allow six weeks for a reply.

To all those hopefuls who are committed, not dysfunctional, like to cuddle, take long walks on the beach, enjoy fine dining, frequent movies, museums and concerts, who come to a relationship with no baggage (maybe a little) and who can afford to buy this book!

ACKNOWLEDGMENTS

Special thanks to Deborah Werksman, our publisher, who shared our vision; to Bob Markel, our literary agent; and to our friends—Melvin Adelglass, John Cocchi and John Springer, who generously gave permission to use their celebrity images.

GUIDE TO ANCIENT PERSONALS SHORTHAND

Sinaitic	Ugaritic	South-Semitic

GAT: Gay African Tribesman

SWS: Single White Slave

DN: Divorced Neanderthal

MAH: Middle-aged Hebrew

LSN: Legally Separated Nubian

SWP: Swinging White Pagan

WBT: Widowed Babylonian Teen

AA: Aged Aramaic

SMB: Single Mesopotamian Brute

BEB: Black Egyptian Bachelor

BO: Bisexual Oriental

BWS: Byzantine Wife Swapper

AE: Annulled Etruscan

SPA: Single Phoenician

PAA: Pre-Adolescent Aborigine

Adam

First man on earth. Age unknown, seeks romantic, passionate person, preferably female, to start human race. I seek someone anatomically similar, yet different, to begat with me in my garden apartment. I'm Jewish (but you needn't be). It's all new to me, but I know what to do...I watch the animals all day long.

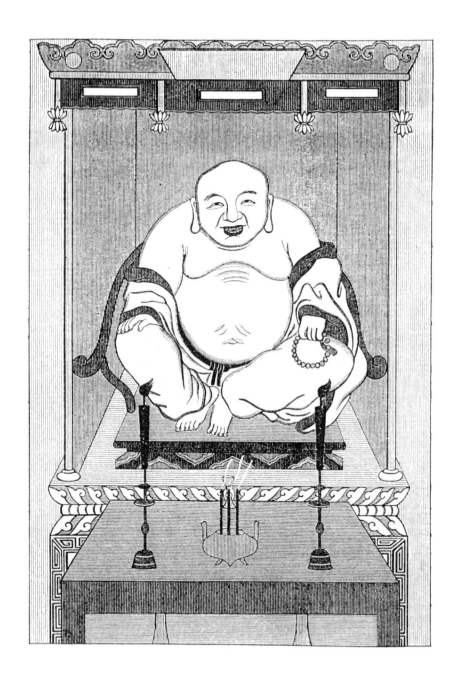

Buddha

This Bud's for you. I'm variously known as Siddhartha and Gautama, but you can call me Bud. The answer to my prayers: a well-endowed woman—about 22 years of age—with a marketing or advertising background to sit on the floor of a cave in India in the lotus position for six years dreaming of marketing plans to promote my books Buddha's 7 Essential Steps to Spiritual Success and How to Satisfy a Buddha Every Time . . . and Have Him Beg for More. I'm really worth the trip. I give great meditation and you'll reach the state of Nirvana. (No EST graduates, please.)

Shiva

I'd like to get my hands on you. Indian love goddess (name withheld) would like to strum her lute and spend lots of your loot at the Taj Mahal (Vegas or Atlantic City). Please be hand-some, hand-y, hale and hardy. I'd like to curry favor with you after a spirited game of hand-ball. People tell me I'm a real hand-ful and can send shiva's up your spine. We can have a wonderful life, Vishnu were here. No Hari Krishnas or Branch Davidians, please.

Confucius

Wonton woman wanted. Answer this ad and Sunday night we could be eating take-out! Humble philosopher seeks little dumpling, sweet or sour, for relationship that will last. In the meal of life, love is a combination platter; never pu-pu the right dish when it comes along. It is better to eat family style than alone at the singles' counter. I could be mild or spicy, and you could be my fortune cookie!

Cleopatra

Sick of the singles scene. This needy, lonely love goddess who always seems to go "home alone" desperately seeks someone she has something Tut-in-kamen with. (My girlfriends put me up to this as I'm too famous to make the "barge" scene.) Please be divine—a pharaoh or a doctor—ready to spend lots of papyrus. My special guy should be animated, not a sphinx, and available for immediate commitment (I've already booked the hall and band). Please believe in marriage at first sight.

Constantine

Great head (of state). My Roman days are over. This all-powerful emperor is now in the market for a classy woman to marry. Introduce me to this woman, and I will pay the finder 100,000 drachmas (up front). She could be your wife, your daughter, your bubba (or mine). Who am I? First Emperor of Rome. Prior to ascending the throne, I was Byzantium's first mall developer (voted top salesman, two years running). Who had time for romance? Now I'm fully rented and ready for lusty former pagan woman who enjoys fine dining and is prepared to relocate to Constantinople (not Istanbul). Age unimportant, but prefer under 16.

Joan of Arc

Gimme vices, not voices. No more torch songs for this SFRF (single French religious fanatic), crowding 16. Forget my holier than thou appearance. I can be a thunderball of passion for that certain guy, preferably a firefighter.

Botticelli's Venus

Sole mate sought. Saucy underwater beauty looking to dredge up mature Renaissance man ready to embark on long-term commitment. In this sea of humanity, I know I have passed you at low tide. My passions include, but are not limited to: swimming, sunbathing, and collecting shells. I love scarfing down seafood, particularly clams oreganata (but you need not) and guys in sharkskin suits. Favorite flick: On the Waterfront. If we click, I would like to fillet you (but not on the first date). No jail bait or fishy replies. This is a sincere offer.

Henry VIII of England

Lady Killer! Seeking princess type for short-term but exciting marriage. We may never grow old together, but while it lasts, this Defender of the Faith will treat you like a Queen. I may be a serial husband (I never met a woman I didn't marry) and a control freak, but I possess a heart (with a pace-maker) full of love. Please be a Norman or Saxon with a great figure, not possessive, who likes living on the cutting edge. You may lose your life, but there'll always be an England!

Mona Lisa

Looks are deceiving. Don't let this enigmatic smile fool you. This demure, shy, delicate SWF who wants a picket fence and a house full of kids is also a passionate hellcat who will try anything once, maybe twice. Please be a renaissance mensch, doctor or lawyer, who shares my love for candlelit dinners, art and museums. You'll find me hanging out at the Louvre.

Christopher Columbus

Clear the decks! Daring, high-spirited explorer about to embark on long trip by sea to discover America seeks first mate. This is no bunk. My first lady on the sea of love will be curvaceous (not scur-vaceous). This is not a luxury cruise, but the company is first class. Plus, you get an extra 10,000 frequent sailor miles. Trousseau should be completely waterproof and rain repellent. Please send a contour map of yourself.

Sir Walter Raleigh

Dandy relationship sought. I want a comely wench with impeccable manners, someone I would lay down my cape for. Please be eclectic. As for me, despite my high social standing, I still find it amusing to shop at thrift shops, consignment stores and flea markets for antique clothes. No slatterns or sluts, please! I'm dandy and randy, but I do have standards. If we get it on, we can travel around the Cape of Good Hope and possibly settle in Capetown.

William Shakespeare

Where are all the great maidens?

England's greatest poet/playwright looking for a Juliet to whom he can play Romeo. If you agree that romance is more than Much Ado About Nothing, why not meet between the acts at the Theatre in the Park? I'll be the guy eating Goobers and Raisinettes. It could turn out to be a Comedy of Errors, but All's Well that Ends Well.

Pocahontas

Indian Princess seeks Indian Giver. This atypical American Princess (20 but looks 10 years younger) is willing to remove warpaint for a man with a good scalp for business to invest in a casino on tribal land. Be tall, dark and Cherokee and love me without reservations. Be stable. No Indian nuts, please. If we hit the romantic jackpot, let's just have snake eyes for each other. Pre-tribal agreement necessary. Just one thing — I hate Westerns.

Wolfgang Amadeus Mozart

Cosi Fan Cutie wanted. Child prodigy, now in early 30's, hopelessly immature, impractical, gross and brilliant, would like to score with comely, shapely, hot tomato (preferably mid-teens) possessing hourglass figure. Think of me as writing within the framework of classical forms, with perfect mastery of all, always with grace and impeccable taste. My genius is comparable with Beethoven's (but yours needn't be). I expect to live a very long life.

Marie Antoinette

Rye, narcissistic French Aristocrat Woman. Seeks high quality, short-term relationship with lower-crust French peasant, preferably baker. I want the whole wheat, so let's roll around while my oven is hot, and I'll bake your meringue until your cruller does the twist. Dough not as important as ability. No half-baked aristocrats, loafers or seedy types. If this ad stirs up your appetite, let's get together for a baker's dozen (no bun intended).

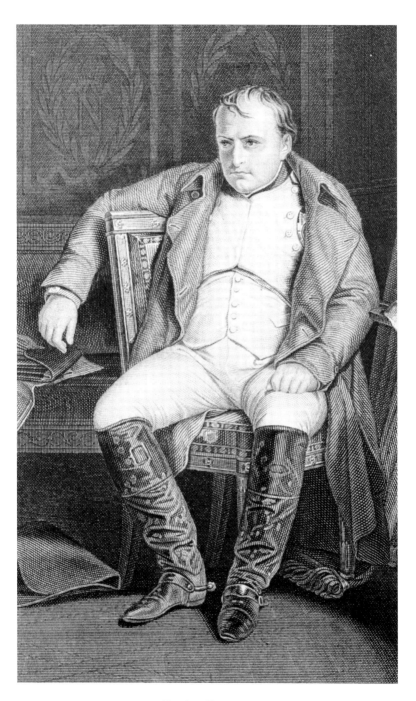

Napoleon Bonaparte

I'd like to go up on you. SWMD (single, white, military dictator), 5'2", now conquering Europe, wants to put special woman, age 16, on pedestal, not under guillotine. My main squeeze is 6' tall, shapely, and a great French kisser. If you possess these qualities and are sincere, prepare to meet your Waterloo with me. Write O. Revoir.

Lady Godiva

Off my high horse. Candy heiress seeks low-sugar daddy for a sincere and tasty relationship, one that won't leave a bad taste in my mouth. No longer seduced by the bittersweet, this lady who is tired of the candy bar scene now refuses cheap imitations created of flat flavorings. I want someone I can nosh on, a Mr. Right with a genuine cocoa base, the kind that dreams are made of...someone hand-dipped and foil-wrapped in a beautiful package. If you're that 50-plus, fun-loving guy with a nutty center, rush candygram and photo. No off-price Whitman Sampler types, please!

Edgar Allen Poe

Novel woman wanted. Take off your Mask of the Red Death, let down your Raven hair and expose me to your Telltale Heart over a Cask of Amontillado at the House of Usher. I am here to give love a chance, not a Premature Burial. Although I come in hardcover, this sensitive author's heart is really a paperback ready to be held and thumbed through by a thrill seeker looking for storybook romance. We'll share figs and grapes, but don't leave pits on my pendulum. Meet me in the fiction section of the library. I'm all yours for three weeks. Thereafter, pay a fine of two pence per day.

Elizabeth Barrett Browning

How do I love thee? Let me count the ways:

1. Money	9. 401k's
2. Income	10. Keogh's
3. Wealth	11. CD's
4. Assets	12. Muni's
5. Bearer Bonds	13. FannieMae's
6. Zero Coupons	14. Silver
7. Gold Bullion	15. Junk Bonds
8. IRA's	

I shall but love thee better after death (when I collect the insurance).

Abraham Lincoln

Trade up to a Lincoln. If you're not happy with your present romantic model, I offer low mileage, high octane, good rubber and a great chassis used only on weekends. Let's take a test drive along a deserted beach where we can wax rhapsodic (Turtle Wax, of course). I have a quick acceleration and I'm great on highways. You: a late model, sleek and streamlined with lots of polish and chrome and glove leather interior. I offer a new lease on life (open or close ended) filled with moving violations. If you are driven to meet the man of your dreams, this ad could be your Emancipation Proclamation!

Charles Dickens

I'll love you like the dickens! I've had the best of dates, I've had the worst of dates. Now I'd like to settle down and share my royalties with the right lady. I'm totally flexible, even if we have to live in two cities. How's this for a twist? Instead of going out to a noisy, trendy tavern, let's sup at my place and I'll read you A Christmas Carol. I'm on the best cellar list (for my wines). This could be the most exciting chapter of your life. P.S. I am completely drug free.

Jules Verne

Seeking a woman in my league(s).
Why pay the single supplement? I want a permanent companion in the trip of life, someone whose taken all her shots and loves champagne and quinine. I have a marvelous travel agent who can procure really great trips: Around the World (in 80 Days), expeditions 20,000 Leagues Under the Sea, and exotic adventures to Mysterious Islands. This ad is not science fiction. I've been married before, but that's water under the bridge. All I want today is to kick off my flippers and relax with a woman who doesn't want to just tread water.

Clara Barton

I'd like to hold your bedpan. Tender, loving, early 20th century nurse (you may recognize my name) wishes to give up co-dependent existence for someone who will infect my heart with true love. Now seeking doctor in private practice for lifetime commitment (no HMO's!!). Please be emotionally available, between the ages of 20 and 70, and either single or widowed (any race or religion). I'm pretty (aorta be in pictures) and ready for major medical if you give me fever in the morning, evening, and all through the night. Interests include moonlight walks through hospital corridors and romantic dinners in the basement cafeteria. Send X-rays, and be patient.

Sherlock Holmes

Fingerprints 'Я' us. Help me solve "The Case of the Missing Woman." This world-renowned detective who has out-witted the greatest criminal minds has eluded that special woman missing from his life. To solve this case I must divest myself of deductive reasoning and instead employ seductive reasoning. Preliminary interview with my associate Watson. According to your rap-sheet, you are 5'2" with eyes of blue, friendly, but not easy and without fear of being investigated. I may fingerprint you while we are holding hands. Have an unblemished record—no shoplifting or crimes of passion.

Jesse James

WANTED! A feisty little gal from the east who isn't stuck-up and is open to a new and different lifestyle. Join my gang and live life to its fullest. We'll take long train rides, meet lots of bank managers and tellers, not to mention train conductors. You'll enjoy life on the Brinks with me and my brother Frank (he's also looking to be fixed up). Rob my heart as you cover my rear and you're all mine in buttons and bows (and bullet-proof vests). No Ma Barker types, please.

P.T. Barnum

Do you have the guts (to love a man like me)? Imagine: being shot out of a cannon or being swung by your hair...500 feet above the Big Top! Flamboyant showman wants leading lady to star in the greatest show on earth. Please be petite (under 3'6") or statuesque (over 7') with flowing locks and a beard. (I could also get attached to siamese twins or a two-headed woman.) We'll create our own dog and pony act and have a freaky-deaky time on my home trapeze (think of it as a romantic NordicTrack). Please include DNA with photo; this is a sincere offer. Send in the clowns!

Vincent van Gogh

I've painted myself into a corner, romantically. I'm canvassing Holland and France for a sophisticated, urban model type to spend many a starry night with me. We can go Dutch. My friends say I am hard to please, that when it comes to commitment I am yellow, but for the right woman—someone with a bright palette and a cleft chin—I could go for the Big "M" (mauve). Critics suggest I am unstable, physically unfit, an erotomaniac and a heavy drinker, but they are just a bunch of old fuddy-duddies. If you do call, would you mind speaking a little louder, please?

Alexander Graham Bell

Call me. This charming inventor of the telephone won't put you on hold. Talk is cheap, but I'm not. Ready to reach out and touch someone, I will go to long distances for you. Please deposit another 25 cents for the next 10 minutes and we can sprint to the altar and have lots of baby bells. Warning: I have caller I.D. No hangups please.

Thomas Alva Edison

Live wire wanted. Looking for a bright woman (soft white or soft pink) who can turn me on and be the light of my life (AC only). I'm ready to pull the plug on loneliness. I'd like to fuse with a high energy lady (about 200 watts)— someone with a 3-way bulb to do it with the lights on. My friends say I'm inventive, so I'd like to go on the record: if you can provide a relationship with electricity, send me a wire letting me know what's watt. (I'm good for about 750 hours, or average lumens 1710.)

V.I. Lenin

Socialist climber. Revolutionary leader, commie-tose due to lack of love, seeks that special redhead. I want to create a new order with an upper-class babe who has more than borscht. Someone exciting who will rip off her babushka and is willing to play romantic Russian roulette. I want a comrade for keeps. This is not just pinko propaganda—it's my love manifesto. No liberals or parasitic leeches need apply.

Aga Khan III

Playboy of the eastern world— available. I'm the spiritual leader of millions, but I'm also a man, praying for a gal pal who loves me tender for myself, not my outrageous fortune (antique auto collection, polo ponies, yachts, retinue of 30 and palaces in every principal resort around the world). We'll double with royal swells like my friends the Mosque-owitz's and mecca big wedding including all my other wives (love is comfortable the 80th time around). I'm tall, dark and handsome with good teeth (several sets). Reach me on my web site, cabana no. 7, or call Friday before sundown.

Harry Houdini

Do you believe in magic? I do. Has love ever left you feeling sawed in half? Then answering this ad could change your life. Just because I'm the world's most famous magician doesn't mean I'll play games with you. I have no tricks up my sleeve. After I've unlocked myself from a padlocked, chain-wrapped trunk at the bottom of the river I end up like any other Joe in a lonely hotel room. I desire a real woman, not an illusion. It would take a special lady to unlock my heart. Send reply to my medium, Mme. Dora.

Amelia Earhart

Come fly with me. I'm willing to take a romantic flyer with a guy who's not on automatic pilot—someone in first class. I want a guy who's willing to go around the world (and not in 80 days), preferably a member of the "Mile High Club." Don't worry about cabin fever-this will be a non-stop flight. We may even go down over Borneo. I can be reached directly, or through your travel agent. Our wedding dinner could consist of fruit plate, seafood, kosher, vegetarian, or other cuisine. (Do phone ahead.)

Albert Einstein

My theory of relativity: $S+E=X^2$.
Now let me explain the basic laws of gravitation and magnetism. In lay terms, the mass (of the woman I seek) will be leggy and busty, times the square speed of light (candlelight in this case). You don't have to be a genius to get it. This theorem is basic to the understanding of the transformation of talk into movement. In other words, action talks. Let's meet and reshape the concept of the universe over a schnapps. If we click, we'll never be divided and we'll multiply like crazy!

Winston Churchill

In my prime. These are perilous times. Let's take shelter at 10 Downing Street (where I have a queen-sized bed). Please be a plucky playmate with wit and honor. We could enjoy our finest hours together—on land, on the sea and in the air. My romantic ally should be an older woman (in her 30's) who is a conservative (although you could wind up in Labour). If we go all the way we'll honeymoon in exotic places like Yalta, Tripoli, and Dunkirk. Let's meet near the white cliffs of Dover for tea and crumpets. Lest we lose our way due to an air raid, we'll meet again (don't know where, don't know when). Here, honey, have a cigar.

General George Patton

Patton pending. Atten-HUT! Bold, audacious, single military leader seeks to do an "about face" and join forces with plucky woman in command of her emotions (mealy mouthed crybabies need not apply). Be tough, aggressive, fearless, yet capable of great passion. How you make love not as important as how you make war. I'm handsome (people tell me I look like George C. Scott) and trim, 'though I'm always fighting the battle of the bulge. Nothing is too good for my non-commissioned female. Awaiting your immediate response. That's an order!

Eva Perón

Can you tapas this? Gorgeous, lonely widow of Argentinian dictator/strongman wishes to overthrow state of loneliness and dance tango of lust with strong, dominant male, who makes my heart go Tico-Tico. My prisoner of love will be personally strip searched and sentenced to a lifetime of love. Religion unimportant. I'm from Argentina (but you needn't be). Interests include self-adornment (my mantra is "jewelry") and long, romantic walks around the barracks. South America, take it away!

Lassie

Let's do it doggie-style. Famous canine film star, housebroken and paper-trained, seeks non-neutered melan-collie baby to make me sit up and beg. Although my paw prints are preserved for posterity at Graumann's Chinese Theatre, I'm still searching for that special some-one to muzzle with in my mansion-sized doghouse. Please be attractive—no mutts. My hobbies: knocking over gar-bage cans, nipping at postmen, slurping cappuccino at Spago. Favorite flick: Ingmar Bergman's The Seventh Seal. Hope I'm not barking up the wrong tree.

Sigmund Freud

Fear of intimacy. Running a personal ad fills me with guilt, discomfort and self-loathing. I am plagued with anxiety; it is increasingly difficult just to leave the house. I know my mother would disapprove (I have no recollection of my father). But enough about you. My recurrent dream girl wants to know all about me and admires cigars, sausages, zucchini and trains rushing through tunnels. If you qualify, call to make an appointment.

Index

Index

Questions Frequently Asked About Personal Ads

Q. Has anyone met through the ads?

A. Many have met.

Q. Do people tell the truth?

A. Never.

Q. Is it true that men are only "out for one thing"?

A. Yes.

Q. Can I meet a doctor?

A. Only if you're taken to the hospital.

Q. Am I responding to ads because of low self-esteem?

A. Yes.

Q. Am I placing my ad because of low self-esteem?

A. Yes.

Q. If I am over 60 years of age, how old should I say I am?

A. 36.

Q. How can I verbalize that I am a nymphomaniac?

A. Very carefully.

Phrases That Turn People On
(and their real meanings)

— I'm financially secure (entering Chapter 11).

— I'm emotionally available (the Lithium is working).

— I'm cuddly (a real tramp).

— I'm a mensch (a real tramp).

— I'm a real woman (not an inflatable plastic doll).

— I'm Jewish (substitute Catholic, Protestant, Buddhist) but you needn't be (I'm not serious, so what's the difference).

— I'm fun-loving (manic-depressive — watch out).

— I'm a woman of substance (not money; substance abuse).

— I'm in the arts (be prepared to eat in).

— I'm the guy of your dreams (ever hear of "Freddy Kruger"?).

— I'm a professional (hooker).

— I have a willing heart (just had triple bypass).

— I'll make you laugh all night long (no sex).

Positive Buzzwords*

— affluent

— loaded

— high tax bracket

— ultra rich venture capitalist

— rich and famous

— heiress

— successful

— wildly successful

— handsome, charming and successful

— successful with multiple achievements

— intelligent, funny and successful

— successful and unencumbered (but you needn't be)

— successful with beach house

— successful and wanting a lasting relationship

*Anything to do with sex or money.

Negative Buzz Words*

— desperate

— bankrupt

— needy

— tormented

— disturbed

— discouraged

— nervous, high strung

— co-dependent

— dysfunctional

— controlling

— introspective

— soulful

— withdrawn

— depressed

— suicidal

* Dangerous to your romantic agenda.

A "Personals" Wish List

— I want a friend.

— I want a good friend.

— I want a best friend.

— I want a dependent friend.

— I want a co-dependent friend.

— I want an independent friend (who can be co-dependent).

— I want a passionate friend.

— I want a friend I can dominate.

— I want a friend who can dominate me.

— I want a friend in need.

— I want a friend indeed.

Danger Signs on the Super Highway to Love

Beware of ads which contain the following ...

— I'm co-dependent.

— I'm independent (when I'm not co-dependent).

— My husband (wife) was seriously neurotic.

— Overlong ads, 15 lines or more (you only want a "meaningful relationship," not to lease a Lexus).

— Use of strange age ranges, like 25-75.

— Use of word "generous."

— People who refer to their beach house, boats, or "wet basements."

— People with overly specific demands (a ploy to hide co-dependency).

— Requests for photos or photocopies of your private parts.

— Getting personal too fast.

Author Harold Rand, a SWM—tall, blonde and frequently mistaken for Kevin Costner—likes to take long walks on secluded beaches, is a published author and a Hollywood film studio public relations executive. Anything but dysfunctional, Rand is a gossip columnist for the New York Friars Club, a leading entertainment institution. When he is not pursuing a meaningful relationship with a high-energy, tempestuous, Reubenesque female in her early to late 20s, he performs as a stand-up humorist. An earlier Rand tome, *The Bowery on $.75 a Day*, was co-written with Robert Saffron and published by Pocket Books.

Doris Chelmow, SWF, has been in the advertising field for 18 years and has won numerous awards for creative writing. She has also authored several articles on manners and morals, most notably the advisory "How to Lie About Your Age." In between shopping, manicures and viewing re-runs of "The Equalizer," the slim and shapely millionairess is adding final touches to a cat humor book. Ms. Chelmow has been pursued by men on four continents, from Brooklyn to Buenos Aires, and can say "no" in 17 languages. She loathes long walks in the country.

Other titles from Hysteria Publications:

BOOKS

- *Getting In Touch with Your Inner Bitch* by Elizabeth Hilts (paperback, $7.95)
- *The Noisy Passage: Baby Boomers Do Menopause* by Marie Evans and Ann Shakeshaft (paperback, $8.95)
- *A Useless Guide to WindBlows95* by Murkysoft (paperback, $7.95)
- *Pandemonium: Or, Life with Kids*, a collection of parental humor (paperback, $8.95)
- *'Cause I'm the Mommy (That's Why!)* by Donna Black (paperback, $7.95)

CALENDARS

- *Personally Yours, A Personal Ads Parody Calendar for 1997* by Doris Chelmow and Harold Rand ($12.95)
- *Sylvia's Cosmic Companion: A Guide to Keeping Your Goddess Happy, Astrological Cartoon Engagement Calendar for 1997* by Nicole Hollander ($12.95)
- *Sylvia's Cosmic Companion: Let the Goddess Run Your Life in 1997, An Astrological Cartoon Wall Calendar* by Nicole Hollander ($12.95)

To place an order, call us at (800) 784-5244.